One Heartbeat At A Time

SONG BY STEVEN CURTIS CHAPMAN

ZONDERVAN®

ZONDERVAN

One Heartbeat At A Time
Copyright © 2010 by Zondervan

Requests for information should be addressed to:
Zondervan, *Grand Rapids, Michigan 49530*

ISBN 978-0-310-51998-0

One Heartbeat At A Time
Written by Steven Curtis Chapman
Copyright © 2005 Sparrow Song (BMI) (adm. by EMI CMG Publishing) /
Peach Hill Songs (BMI) All rights reserved. Used by permission.

Cover design by Holli Leegwater | HL Design
Interior design by Holli Leegwater & Michelle Espinoza

Printed in China

09 10 11 12 13 14 15 • 20 19 18 17 16 15 14 13 12 11 10 9 8 7 6 5 4 3 2 1

One Heartbeat At A Time

by Steven Curtis Chapman

You're up all night with a screaming baby
You run all day at the speed of life
And every day you feel a little bit less
Like the beautiful woman you are

So you fall into bed when you run out of hours
And you wonder if anything worth doing got done
Well, maybe you just don't know
Or maybe you've forgotten

You, you are changing the world
One little heartbeat at a time
Making history with every touch and every smile
Oh, you, you may not see it now
But I believe that time will tell
How you, you are changing the world
One little heartbeat at a time

With every "I know you can do it"
And every tear that you kiss away
So many little things that seem to go unnoticed
They're just like the drops of rain
Over time they become a river

You're beautiful
So beautiful
How you're changing the world
Yeah, you're changing the world

One Heartbeat At A Time
—How the Song Came to Be

"Record it! Record it!" the audience chanted when Steven Curtis Chapman first sang "One Heartbeat At A Time," and so he did. But the song almost didn't see the light.

Chapman explained that whenever he is on tour—which is often—he calls home at night after the concert to talk to his wife Mary Beth, ask her about her day and wish her goodnight. When "One Heartbeat At A Time" was written, the Chapmans had four children at home and there was always noise in the background—a wailing child or some other distraction. Mary Beth would often sound frazzled, and one night she told Steven she felt she hadn't accomplished much that day. But Steven knew that acts that seemed insignificant to a busy mother really were changing the world one heartbeat at a time. And so after they said goodnight, he began writing the lyrics to "One Heartbeat At A Time" to honor, he says, not only his wife, but all mothers.

Steven finished the lyrics that night and later composed the music on the piano. But then the song lay "in the bottom of my guitar case" for a while. Eventually a country

music singer friend recorded the song but it was not released. Then in 2007 Steven remembered the song and thought it would be a great addition to a performance at a Women of Faith conference. He doesn't remember the city where the conference was held but he clearly remembers performing the song. When he finished he heard voices coming from the audience and, listening closely, he realized they were chanting something. And then he made out their words: "Record it! Record it!" Obviously, the song had a tremendous impact on the 15,000 women present that evening. And it continues to resonate with Christian women everywhere, for they are truly "changing the world."

Steven Cole

You're up all night with a screaming baby
You run all day at the speed of life
And every day you feel a little bit less
Like the beautiful woman you are

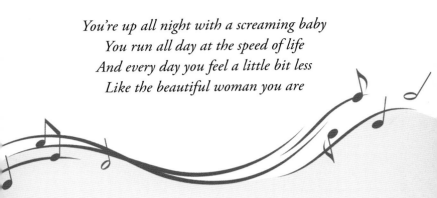

Beauty is the mark God sets upon virtue.

Ralph Waldo Emerson

God has made everything beautiful in its time.

Ecclesiastes 3:11

The unfading beauty of a gentle and quiet spirit …
is of great worth in God's sight.

1 Peter 3:4

So you fall into bed when you run out of hours
And you wonder if anything worth doing got done

No Neurosis

Other girls have ropes of pearls,
    Other girls wear mink;
I have ropes of drying clothes,
    And dishes in the sink.

Other girls drive sporty cars,
    Other girls have maids;
I must steer a shopping cart,
    And eat meat's cheaper grades.

Other girls rely on cards
    To fill the empty hours;
I have noses to be wiped,
    No time for sulks and glowers

Other girls use beauty parlors
    To keep them in the pink;
A laughing child and a husband's arms
    Are better aids, I think.

                    Florence Bell Williams

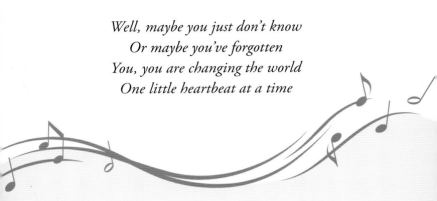

Well, maybe you just don't know
Or maybe you've forgotten
You, you are changing the world
One little heartbeat at a time

I do dimly perceive that while everything around me is ever
changing, ever dying, there is underlying all that change
a living power that is changeless, that holds all together, that
creates, dissolves, and recreates. That informing power of spirit is
God, and since nothing else that I see merely through the senses
can or will persist, he alone is.

Mohandas K. Gandhi

Nothing endures but change.

Heraclitus

It is personalities, not principles, that move the age.

Oscar Wilde

Making history with every touch and every smile

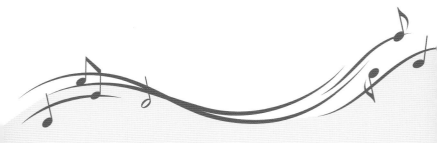

The best effect of fine persons
is felt after we have left their presence.

Ralph Waldo Emerson

Blessed is the influence of one true, loving soul on another.

George Eliot

Every life is a profession of faith,
and exercises an inevitable and silent influence.

Henri Frederic Amiel

Oh, you, you may not see it now
But I believe that time will tell
How you, you are changing the world
One little heartbeat at a time

In some cultures, clouds, especially white ones, are symbols of great importance, and their movement signifies the impermanence of all things. Watching clouds move across the sky, it is easy to see how subtly they can change and have a different and often significant effect on the ground below. Sometimes a storm blows in quickly, but more often the clouds drift lazily by. Observe one pattern, look away for a second and the pattern has changed almost imperceptibly but it has nevertheless changed. Some tiny gust from somewhere has affected what the world below sees and experiences. For example, in my native Michigan it is a fact of life that the weather in Wisconsin will be here tomorrow. The weather in Minnesota will be here, too. It will just take a day longer.

If simple air currents can, by their movement, have such an impact on our lives, think how the tiniest, most humble acts of a human can have so much more effect. Will an act of kindness from one person to another in Minneapolis or Milwaukee somehow ripple through the words and deeds of others to arrive at my door in Michigan? I believe it will, and my world will be changed for the better.

Steven Cole

With every "I know you can do it"

Whenever we do what we can,
we immediately can do more.

James Freeman Clarke

Do thou thy best, and leave to God the rest.

James Howell

Always give yourselves fully to the work of the Lord,
because you know that your labor in the
Lord is not in vain.

1 Corinthians 15:58

And every tear that you kiss away

We find great things are made of little things,
And little things go lessening till at last
Comes God behind them.

Robert Browning

The hand that rocks the cradle
Is the hand that rules the world.

William Ross Wallace

O Lord, you will keep us safe.

Psalm 12:7

So many little things that seem to go unnoticed

There's a well-trodden path
From nursery to sink
From eternal nocturnally
Fetching his drink.

Pat Cunningham

Do you know what mommies do
While they stay at home with you? …

They are busy all day through,
And here's a little secret,
Moms are busiest
Loving you!

Lonnie Carton

No man is poor who has a godly mother.

Abraham Lincoln

They're just like the drops of rain
Over time they become a river

Life is a succession of moments
To live each one is to succeed.

Corita Kent

Mother's love is ever in its spring.

French proverb

Heaven is at the feet of mothers.

Persian proverb

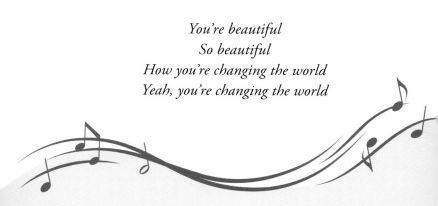

You're beautiful
So beautiful
How you're changing the world
Yeah, you're changing the world

Whenever I held my newborn baby in my arms, I used to think that what I said and did to him could have an influence not only on him but on all whom he met, not only for a day or a month or a year, but for all eternity—a very, very challenging and exciting thought for a mother.

Rose Kennedy

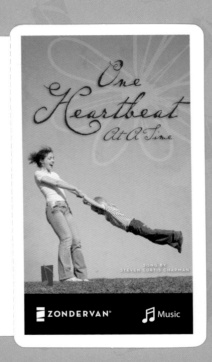

One Heartbeat At A Time

SONG BY
STEVEN CURTIS CHAPMAN

ZONDERVAN®   ♫ Music